ORPHEUS

by the same author

poetry
NIL NIL
GOD'S GIFT TO WOMEN
THE EYES
LANDING LIGHT

aphorism
THE BOOK OF SHADOWS

editor
101 SONNETS
ROBERT BURNS: SELECTED POEMS
LAST WORDS (with Jo Shapcott)
DON'T ASK ME WHAT I MEAN (with Clare Brown)
NEW BRITISH POETRY (with Charles Simic)

Orpheus

A version of Rilke's
Die Sonette an Orpheus

DON PATERSON

faber and faber

First published in 2006
by Faber and Faber Limited
3 Queen Square London WC1N 3AU
This paperback edition published in 2007

Typeset by Faber and Faber and Faber Limited
Printed in England by T. J. International Ltd, Padstow, Cornwall

A CIP record for this book
is available from the British Library

ISBN 978-0-571-22270-4

2 4 6 8 10 9 7 5 3 1

For Annie

Contents

PART ONE

Orpheus, 3
Girl, 4
A God, 5
The Spaces, 6
Leaving, 7
The Double Realm, 8
Praising, 9
Lament, 10
Tone, 11
The Sarcophagi
    in Rome, 12
Horseman, 13
The Spirit, 14
Taste, 15

The Dead, 16
Orange, 17
Dog, 18
Tree, 19
The Machine, 20
Change, 21
Horse, 22
Spring, 23
The Race, 24
Flight, 25
The Gods, 26
Blood, 27
The Trace, 28

PART TWO

Breath, 31
The Look, 32
Mirror, 33
Unicorn, 34
Anemone, 35
Rose, 36
Cut Flowers, 37
The Ball, 38
Mercy, 39

The Real, 40
The Kill, 41
Change, 42
The Passing, 43
The Flowers, 44
The Drinking Fountain, 45
The Stream, 46
Solace, 47
The Spin, 48

The Beggar, 49
Distance, 50
Gardens, 51
Abundance, 52
The Hour, 53
The Venturers, 54

Cycles, 55
The Cry, 56
Time, 57
Dancer, 58
Being, 59

Afterword, 61
APPENDIX Fourteen Notes on the Version, 73
Acknowledgements, 85

PART ONE

Orpheus

A tree rose from the earth. O pure transcendence –
Orpheus sings: O tall oak in the ear!
All was still. And then within that silence
he made the sign, the change, and touched the lyre.

One by one they crept out from the wood,
emptying each set and form and lair;
and looking in their eyes, he understood
they'd fallen quiet in neither stealth nor fear,

but in their listening. Growl and bark and roar
died in their breast as each took to the clearing.
Before this day, there hadn't been a shack

that might have held the song, a plain earthwork
hollowed by their most obscure desire:
today the temple rises in their hearing.

Girl

Almost a girl . . . Who suddenly took wing
above that wedding of the voice and lyre,
who blazed below the veils of her own Spring
and made herself a bed inside my ear.

And slept in me. And all things were her sleep.
Those tangible eternities – the trees
that took my breath, the meadows, green and deep –
everything that overwhelmed my eyes.

She slept the world. How could you so except
her, singing god, that she did not first
desire to be awake? She arose, and slept.

Where is her death? Will you invent this theme
before your song is over? To what realm
does she sink from me? A girl, almost . . .

A God

A god can do it. But how can a man follow,
will someone tell me, through the narrow lyre?
His mind is cloven. No temple to Apollo
can rise at such a crossroads of desires.

And song is *not* desire; so you taught.
Nor is it courtship, nor is it courtship's prize.
Song is being. Easy for a god.
But when are *we*? When will the Earth and stars

be squandered on us, on *our* living? Youth –
don't fool yourself that love unlocks this art;
for though love's voice might force your lips apart

you must forget those sudden songs. They'll end.
True singing is another kind of breath.
A breath of nothing. A sigh in a god. A wind.

The Spaces

Sometimes, O gentle ones . . . Step outside
into that indifferent breath: letting it break
cold across your face as it divides
to shudder closed again behind your back.

O whole ones, blessed ones: you seem the heart's
initiation and initiative –
crossbow for the dart, target for the dart,
a tearstained smile that nothing can outlive.

Don't fear your suffering. Give up your burden:
the Earth will barely notice its return.
Heavy the mountains, heavier the seas.

Even the trees you planted here as children
have long since grown too heavy to be borne.
Ah, but the winds . . . Ah, but the spaces . . .

Leaving

Raise no stone to his memory. Just let
the rose put forth each year, for his name's sake.
Orpheus. In time, perhaps he'll take
the shape of this, and then of that – and yet

we need no other name: *Orpheus*, we say
wherever the true song is manifest.
He comes and goes. Therefore are we not blessed
if he outlasts the flowers a few days?

But though his constant leaving is a torment,
leave he must, if we're to understand.
So even as his voice alters the moment,

he's already gone where no one can pursue;
even the lyre cannot ensnare his hands.
And yet in this defiance, he stays true . . .

The Double Realm

Does he belong here? No, his spacious nature
had its birth in both realms. Who has dwelt
among the willow's roots will weave the osier
so much more deftly in the upper light.

When you pinch the candles, never leave the bread
or milk out on the table; the famished shades
are drawn by them. But he can *raise* the dead,
and conjured through his half-transparent lids

confuses that dark land in everything:
the lore of earth-smoke, meadow-rue and may
appear as real to him as their bright bloom.

Nothing can diminish the true emblem.
Whether lifted from the hearth or the cold clay,
let him praise the pitcher, torque and ring.

Praising

Praising, that's it! One appointed to praise –
he came like the ore from the stone,
its locked silence . . . His quick heart, a tireless press
for that wine, eternal to man.

His voice never dries or fails when the divine
grips him to pour from his mouth –
and everything turns to vineyard and vine,
ripe in his aesthetic South.

Nothing can prove him untrue when he sings:
not the mould on the tombs of the kings,
nor the gods' shadowfall.

He is holding deep into the doors of the dead
the prizes, the fruit-laden bowls:
the herald who stayed.

Lament

Lament, our naiad of the weeping spring:
only in the praise-realm may she walk –
to watch over our tearfall, our own raining,
that it might run clear on the very rock

which raises up the altars and tall gates.
Look: around her silent shoulders dawns
the understanding that she came here late,
that of the sisters, she is the last-born.

Joy knows it all, while Longing just confesses.
But night on night her small hands weigh and sift
the ancient evil as she learns the truth.

And yet – awkward and artless – she will lift
the sudden constellation of our voices
into a sky unclouded by her breath –

Tone

Only one who's also raised
his lyre among the shades
may live to render up the praise
that cannot fail or fade.

Only one who tasted death's
own flower on his lips
can keep that tone as light as breath
beneath his fingertips.

Though its reflection starts to swim
before your failing sight:
know the image.

Only in the double realm
is the voice both infinite
and assuaged.

The Sarcophagi in Rome

Old tombs, you never leave me long.
Your heavy lids still guard their dreams:
the murmurs of the ancient streams
roll on like half-remembered songs.

Though some have woken, their black eyes
as wide as shepherds': all deadnettle
and stillness, filling with the petals
of new-hatched, bone-white butterflies.

I praise all things wrested from doubt.
Those mouths alive with their new voice
having learnt the truth of silence.

So do we know it, or do we not?
This question is the hesitance
that tolls in every human face.

Horseman

Look at the sky: is there no constellation
called *The Horseman*? Because this is our song –
a beast's will, and some higher distillation
steering and braking as it's borne along.

Isn't this just our sinewy existence,
spurring ourselves on, reining ourselves back in?
Track and turning; then one touch – a new distance
opens up, and the two are one again.

But is that true? Don't they just signify
the road they take together? As it is,
they're sundered by the table and the trough.

Even their starry union is a lie.
For now, we can do nothing but insist
we read it there. And maybe that's enough.

The Spirit

Praise the spirit that can make us one,
for we live our lives in signs and figures. Truly:
the false clocks with their little steps march on
beside the stream of our authentic day.

And though our element's a mystery
we somehow still act out of what it marries –
antennae seeking out other antennae
as the empty distance carries . . .

Pure tension. O harmony of the powers!
Do we keep you free from chaos, somehow bleed
it off in all our frantic intercourse?

For what, the farmer's fuss and fret? The sower
can't reach down to where the fattening seed
is turning towards summer. The Earth *bestows*.

Taste

Gooseberry, banana, pear
and apple, all the ripenesses . . .
Read it in the child's face:
the life-and-death the tongue hears

as she eats . . . This comes from far away.
What is happening to your mouth?
Where there were words, discovery
flows, all shocked out of the pith –

What we call *apple* . . . Do you dare
give it a name? This sweet-sharp fire
rising in the taste, to grow

clarified, awake, twin-sensed,
of the sun and earth, the here and the now –
the sensual joy, the whole Immense!

The Dead

Our business is with fruit and leaf and bloom.
Though they speak with more than just the season's
    tongue –
the colours that they blaze from the dark loam
all have something of the jealous tang

of the dead about them. What do we know of their part
in this, those secret brothers of the harrow,
invigorators of the soil – oiling the dirt
so liberally with their essence, their black marrow?

But here's the question: are the flower and fruit
held out to us in love, or merely thrust
up at us, their masters, like a fist?

Or are *they* the lords, asleep amongst the roots,
granting to us in their great largesse
this hybrid thing – part brute force, part mute kiss?

Orange

Wait . . . That taste, that fugitive song –
a half-melody, a tapped foot, a low hum . . .
Ah, girls . . . Young women, so silent, so warm –
dance it, dance what you know on your tongue!

One taste of the orange . . . After that, who
could forget how it drowns in itself, yet resists its
own sweetness? But look, you have caught it,
    possessed it –
its taste, now deliciously changed into you . . .

Now dance it, its dream of the South, let it go
whirling from you, that its bright orb might glow
in its native winds once again! Blushing, releasing

perfume on perfume – to know yourself kin
with the light-pored, pure and stubborn skin,
the juice that fills the whole fruit to rejoicing!

Dog

My dumb friend . . . You are so alone
because of us, each word and sign
we use to make this world our own –
the fraction that we should decline.

But can we point towards a scent?
You know the powers that threaten us.
You bark out when the dead are present;
you shrink back from the spell and curse.

These broken views we must pretend
form the whole and not the part.
Helping you will be difficult

and never plant me in your heart –
I'd grow too fast. But I'd guide his hand,
saying: *Here. This is Esau in his pelt.*

Tree

Bound in the roots, the source
of our slow rise: The Ancient,
the unacknowledged force
that drives our blind ascent –

hunter's horn and warpath,
the proverbs of the elders,
men locked in their brother-wrath,
the women like guitars . . .

But the branches knot and hook
limb on limb . . . Get clear,
just one . . . O climb, climb higher!

And still they break. But look:
the topmost of them shears,
bends into a lyre –

The Machine

Do you hear the New, master?
Its droning and revving,
its prophets arriving,
its scribes and broadcasters –

In all this upheaval
no ear can stay true;
yet each wing-nut and screw
still craves your approval.

Look how the machines
conspire to unnerve us –
deform and demean us,

their cry – *You deserve us* . . .
No. Cold and serene,
let them still. Let them serve us.

Change

The world can no more keep its form
than a cloud can in the sky;
yet all perfected things fall home
to their antiquity.

Above the changing and the dead,
freer, wider, higher –
your first song still rings on ahead,
O god with the lyre.

Our pain still comes as a surprise;
our love has not been learned;
the very reason for our death

stays wholly undiscerned.
Only the song above the Earth
hallows and glorifies.

Horse

What shall I offer you, lord, what homage,
who gave the creatures their ear?
I remember one Spring, in Russia . . .
It was evening, and at the first star

a white horse
crossed the village square, one fetlock hobbled
for a night alone in the field . . .
And how his ticking mane exactly followed

his great heart, its high-swung
drumbeat – cantering as if that crude shackle
did not exist . . . How the fountains of his blood

leapt! That horse knew the distances – how he sang,
and listened! Your myth-cycle
was closed in him. I'll dedicate his image.

Spring

The waking Earth, on this Spring morning
is a child with her poems all memorized;
so many poems . . . She takes the prize
for all the trouble of her learning.

Her teacher was strict. We loved the snow
in the old man's beard . . . And if anyone
should ask what we call the blue or the green,
she knows it – she'll answer, she knows!

O happy Earth, O Earth on holiday,
play with your children! Let us try
to catch you . . . The happiest always will.

All he taught her, the thousand things
printed through the roots, the tall,
difficult stalks . . . She sings them, she sings!

The Race

Man is the driver.
But time and speed
in the weave of forever
are twists in a thread:

what races or flies
is already over.
We're already baptised
in the endless river.

So boys, don't waste
your courage on time-
trials, or test-flights –

all these are at rest:
darkness and light;
the book and the bloom.

Flight

Only when flight
no longer draws
into those blue heights
for its own lost cause

but to play the wind's lass,
gracile and pliant
and sure – nothing less
than the pure instrument . . .

Not till that pure *whither*
takes him beyond
his boy's machine-love

will he know what to prove
and outstrip the weather
to be his flight's end

The Gods

Shall we now forswear our oldest friendships,
the undemanding gods – because the steel
we trained so hard has made them the less real?
Or should we plot their names on our new maps?

Still strong enough to take our dead, their kind
no longer even brush against our wheels.
We've moved our bathhouses and banquet-halls
too distant, and left their heralds far behind.

Lonelier, so needful of each other, yet
strangers still – these days, we never set
our paths as sweet meanders; we lay them straight.

Only in the great combustion chambers
do the old fires burn, and heave the growing hammers;
but us . . . Our strength is fading now, like swimmers.

Blood

But you . . . You, whom I knew like a flower
whose name I don't know: I'll summon once more
to show them, show how you were taken away,
O beautiful friend of the infinite cry.

But dancer first, who – with what sweet hesitance –
paused, as if casting her girlhood in bronze,
in mourning, in listening – until from some great height
music fell into her altered heart.

Sickness now stalked her, her blood overflowing
with shadows – and yet, caught by only a fleeting
suspicion, rushed into her natural Spring.

But again dark and gravity poisoned its source
till it gleamed of the earth; then, wildly beating,
it roared through the steadily widening doors.

The Trace

But you, divine one – singing to the end
as the swarm of maenads set about your murder,
drowning their screams with pure melodic order.
Amidst its ruin, you built the song again.

Not one could harm your head, or break the lyre
however they raged. Each sharp-edged flint
flung at your heart turned soft as clay the instant
it touched you; then found that it could hear.

Though at the last, their wrath dismantled you
while your voice was taken up by everything,
the lions, rocks, birds and trees. There it still rings.

O lost god, you eternal trace! Only through
your final scattering could we be true
and hear the Earth, to sing of what she sings.

PART TWO

Breath

Breath, you invisible poem –
pure exchange, sister to silence,
being and its counterbalance,
rhythm wherein I become,

ocean I accumulate
by stealth, by the same slow wave;
thriftiest of seas . . . Thief
of the whole cosmos! What estates,

what vast spaces have already poured
through my lungs? The four winds
are like daughters to me.

So do you know me, air, that once sailed
    through me?
You, that were once the leaf and rind
of my every word?

The Look

As only the nearest page is quick enough
to take away the master's truest mark,
so a mirror takes into itself
the smile a girl discloses to the dark

while she sits up on her own to meet the sunrise
or the moonrise, in the candle's silent gaze –
where elsewhere, just a dead reflection flies
back into her real and breathing face.

What *do* the eyes send forth? What looks collude
with the black-and-crimson of the dying hearth?
In every glance, a whole life gone for good.

O who knows all the losses of the Earth?
Only one who would yet praise them all,
and sing his heart out, born into the whole.

Mirror

Mirrors: no one's had the skill
to speak about your secret lives.
Doors cut into time, you're filled
with nothing but the holes of sieves –

squaring the ballroom's emptiness
when the dusk comes on, wide as the woods,
and the chandelier vaults through your face
like a stag across a moonlit road.

Sometimes you're all portraits. A few
have seeped into your skin, though most
are ushered by, and some dismissed –

but the loveliest stay . . . Until the true
Narcissus, free and realised,
dives to take the withheld kiss.

Unicorn

This is the animal that never was.
Not knowing that, they loved it anyway:
its bearing, its stride, its high, clear whinny,
right down to the still light of its gaze.

It never was. And yet such was their love
the beast arose, where they had cleared the space;
and in the stable of its nothingness
it shook its white mane out and stamped its hoof.

And so they fed it, not with hay or corn
but with the chance that it might come to pass.
All this gave the creature such a power

its brow put out a horn; one single horn.
It grew inside a young girl's looking-glass,
then one day walked out and passed into her.

Anemone

In the meadow the anemone
is creaking open to the dawn.
By noon, the sky's polyphony
will flood her white lap till she drowns.

The tiny muscle in her star
is tensed to open to the All,
yet the daylight's blast so deafens her
she barely heeds the sunset's call

or finds the willpower to refurl
her petal-edges – her, the power
and will of how many other worlds!

In our violence, we outlive her.
But which new life will see *us* flower
and face the skies, as true receivers?

Rose

Enthroned one: in the ancient understanding,
you were no more than a cup with a plain rim.
But for us, you are the full-blown, infinite bloom,
the wholly indefatigable thing:

impossible richness, silk dress on silk dress
laid upon a body of pure light –
and yet one naked petal will negate
all attire, all show of outwardness.

Through the centuries, your fragrance spoke
its sweetest word to us, never the same;
suddenly it fills the air, like fame.

Even so, we can't find it a name,
we only guess . . . Then memory starts to smoke
from such old hours as we can still invoke . . .

Cut Flowers

Flowers: kin, in the end, to the hands
(always girls') that arrange you . . . Now feeble,
exhausted, after those softly-dealt wounds,
laid out on the garden table

as you wait for the water to keep your green life
from the sleep, seeping into your languor;
but now, lifted up in the streaming poles, safe
in the sensitive charge of those fingers

that will heal you more than you could ever have
    guessed . . .
O light ones, waking again in the bowl,
slowly cooling, exhaling the warmth and perfume

of girl . . . Like a sin, or that dull sin confessed:
that of your cutting . . . And again we recall
your sisters-in-fate, allies in the bloom.

The Ball

What happened to that little brotherhood,
lords of the scattered gardens of the city?
We were all so shy, I never understood
how we hooked up in the first place; like the lamb

with the scroll that spoke, we too spoke in silence.
It seemed when we were happy it was no one's;
whose ball *was* it? In all the anxiety
of that last summer, it melted in the scrum:

the street leaned like a stage-set, the traffic
rolled around us, like huge toys; nobody
knew us. What was real in that All?

Nothing. Just the ball. Its glorious arc.
Not even the kids . . . But sometimes one, already
fading, stepped below it as it fell.

Mercy

Judges: don't boast that you've no use for torture
and the days of the brand and the shackle have gone.
Not one heart is lightened because some willed rapture
of mercy now tenderly clutches your own.

Whatever the scaffold was fed it would throw
back, as a boy would a toy he had broken.
But how the *real* god of mercy would flow
through the gate of the heart, the heart newly woken:

how much more glorious he'd be in his sway,
how powerfully he would announce his dominion!
More than a wind for the great ships to harness,

and not less than the occult and subtle awareness
gaining us silently from within . . . To play
like a quiet child, born of an infinite union.

The Real

All we've achieved, the machinery threatens
as soon as it thinks itself not slave, but power:
where is the mastery, the fine hesitance
in those raw blocks it cuts for the rational towers?

It won't stop, so we cannot escape it, nor leave it
oiling itself in its hushed factories.
It is the Real, not us – so believes it
does everything better: designs, builds, destroys.

But for us . . . Being here is still magic, a source
with a thousand wellheads; a net of pure force
that no one can touch and not kneel down in awe.

Before the beyond-words, words scatter like straw.
And music still quarries its purposeless space
for the vibrant rock, to build its holy place.

The Kill

Far-conquering man . . . You've written, since you first
turned hunter, many a level new death-rule
of trap or net. Though I know the strip of sail
they hung into the caverns of the Karst,

so softly, like the flag of peace, or ceasefire . . .
Then, at the cave-mouth, the boy gave it a jerk
and tumbling dayward out of the cave-dark
came a handful of pale doves. This too is fair.

No one could take pity on their breath,
least of all those men who raised their sights
and in that wakeful moment understood:

Our wandering sorrow takes the shape of death.
The spirit fallen into quietude
knows that what befalls it must be right.

Change

Seek the transformation. Be hungry for that burning
wherein the thing, proud with its change, will always
   slip your mind –
that terrestrial daemon, that genius of design
who in the figure's arc sits on the still point of its turning.

What's locked into mere *residence* is petrified already;
does it feel safe in its dark cage, with its grey-suited
   guards?
Beware, though: from afar, the hardest comes to warn
   the hard;
and woe to them – the adamantine hammer rises steady!

Who pours himself out as the source: he is known by
   Knowing,
and led by her, enchanted, through the realm of still
   Creation
whose closing is its opening, whose coming is its going.

Each happy space they wander through amazed is
   Difference's
child or grandchild. And Daphne, after her own trans-
   formation
wants you, in her laurel-mood, to change into her
   breeze . . .

The Passing

Be ahead of all departure; learn to act
as if, like the last winter, it was all over.
For among the winters, one is so exact
that wintering it, your heart will last for ever.

Die, die through Eurydice – that you might pass
into the pure accord, praising the more, singing
the more; amongst the waning, be the glass
that shatters in the sound of its own ringing.

Be; and at the same time know the state
of non-being, the boundless inner sky,
that this time you might fully honour it.

Take all of nature, its one vast aggregate –
jubilantly multiply it by
the nothing of yourself, and clear the slate.

The Flowers

Consider the flowers: true only to the earth
yet we lend them a fate, from the borders of fate,
and supervise their fadings, their little deaths.
How right that we should author their regret:

everything rises – and yet we trudge along,
laying our heavy selves upon the world.
What wearisome teachers we are for things!
While the Earth dreams on in its eternal childhood.

But if someone took them into infinite sleep,
lay down with them . . . how lightly he would waken
to the different day, out of the common deep –

or perhaps he'd stay: stay until they weakened
and took him in as one of their own kind,
a meadow-brother, a breath inside the wind.

The Drinking Fountain

O tireless giver, holy cataract,
conductor of the inexhaustible One –
your clear tongue, lifting through the mask of stone
you hold before your face . . . Behind you, aqueducts

vanish into the distance. From the Apennine
foothills, through the wheat fields and the graveyards,
they bear the sacred utterance, the words
that arrive for ever, blackening your chin

to fall into the basin that lies rapt
to your constant murmur, like a sleeping ear.
Marmoreal circumstance. Listening rock.

An ear of Earth's, so she only really talks
to herself. So when we're filling up our pitcher,
it feels to her that someone interrupts.

The Stream

God is the place that always heals over,
however often we tear it. We are so
jagged, as we always have to *know*;
but withholding both his favour and disfavour,

he accepts even the purest of our gifts
with the same indifference and stony calm,
standing motionless to face the rift
our each enquiry opens in his realm.

Listen: that low hissing is the stream
where the dead kneel down to drink
at his mute signal.

We pray to keep it near us, as the lamb
might beg the shepherd for its bell,
from its stillest instinct.

Solace

Where, in what blessed, endlessly irrigated gardens,
    on what trees,
from what delicately unpetalled calyces
do the fruits of solace ripen?
Those rare, superb fruits that you stumble upon

in the trampled meadow of your loss, each new find
a marvel in its size, its firm, smooth rind,
in its somehow escaping the whim
of the bird, the envy of the worm.

Are there trees the angels frequent,
tended by slow gardeners with a secret glamour
such that they bear for us, without belonging to us?

Have we never been able – we ghosts and shadows,
so recklessly ripened, withered and spent –
to disturb the balance of those perfect summers?

The Spin

Dancer: O translator of all passing
into act . . . how you called it down that day!
And how that final pirouette, that flurried tree,
spun the whole year in its wild embracing!

Didn't stillness blossom at the crown,
so a thousand other poses seemed to swarm
around it? And above you, immeasurably warm –
was there not a summer there, a sun?

But your ecstatic tree, it bore its fruit –
isn't this its harvest: the thrown pot
flowering in its stripes, the ripened vase?

And the images . . . How the vision persists
of the dark stroke of your eyebrow, sketched so fast
on the blank page of the blur of your pale face –

The Beggar

Gold lies pampered in its vaults somewhere,
intimate with thousands. But that blind man . . .
like the square of dust below a chair,
a stranger to the very lowest coin.

Gold parades along the High Street shops,
all done up in flowers and silks and furs.
The silent man stands in the silent gaps
between its breathing as it sleeps or stirs.

How does that hand close itself each evening?
Every sunrise, fate sends it abroad –
so frail and luminous, it must amaze

the one who sees it clearly. Let him praise
its dreadful endurance: that only sings
to the singer; that's heard just by the god.

Distance

From star to star – such distances: and yet
those encountered here are harder reckoned.
Someone – a child, say, and then a second . . .
What dark matter holds them separate?

Fate measures us in ways too strange and near
for us to know: by being's secret span.
How many from the woman to the man
whose eyes she can't meet, yet she so desires?

All is distance, every circle broken.
Look at this well-laid table, at that dish –
how strange the eyes and dead mouths of the fish;

we think they have no language. Who can say?
And if they do . . . is there a world where they
are absent, and yet find their tongue still spoken?

Gardens

My heart . . . sing the gardens I can only dream;
clear, unattainable, as if poured in glass,
the lakes and roses of Ispahan, Shiraz –
they have no equal; sing the bliss of them.

My heart . . . show it's those lands you call home,
that it's you they think of, when their figs grow full;
that when their winds grow almost visible,
it's you they embrace in their flowering limbs.

And you must never think you sacrificed
all choice, when you made that one: to be!
Silk thread, you're sewn into the tapestry.

With whatever image forms your inner tryst –
even for one second, in the years of grief –
know, implied there, the whole glorious weave.

Abundance

O, despite our certain fate . . . the bewildering
overflow of our lives! How it pours
over into great parks, stone men shouldering
the balconies, flanking the broad doors;

or the brazen bell that every hour will take
its bludgeon to the dullness of the day,
or that column – that *one* column – in Karnak
outlasting the temples' near-eternity.

Today, those same abundances will race
past us, agents of pure haste – from the blind
white morning to the undark, bloated night.

The frenzy passes off, and leaves no trace.
But they'll live on, those lovely arcs of flight,
and their inscribers. If only in the mind.

The Hour

That hour that always so determinedly
escapes you, you know the one . . . Summon me there:
that hour that looms up, imploringly near
as a dog's sad face, only to turn away

just when you think you've finally brought it home.
But what is thus withdrawn will gift you most.
We are free; we were specifically dismissed
at the place we were most certain of our welcome.

Desperately, we try to find a hold –
too young, sometimes, for what is very old;
too old, sometimes, for what had never been.

Only singing are we just and true –
for then we are at once the axe, the bough
and the sweet and ripening danger in between.

The Venturers

O this desire, from the freshly broken soil!
No one helped them, in those earliest days –
yet the cities rose above the quiet bays
and their pitchers filled with well-water and oil.

Our bold drafts of the gods, Fate so resents
they're sullenly destroyed, time after time.
But surely we should heed their timeless names
since they will hear *us*, in the last event?

One generation, now millennia old –
all parents, heavy with that future child
by whom, one day, we'll find ourselves supplanted.

So endlessly ventured . . . How much time we're granted!
Only tight-lipped death knows our true price,
and how he always profits from our lease.

Cycles

Today, if you listen, you can hear the rough breath
of the early harrows, the human rhythm sing
in the deep ingathered stillness of the earth,
the strong Earth rising in its early Spring . . .

The word is old, but never seems outdated
and every year arrives like something new,
though it has come so often. Always anticipated,
though not once did you catch it. It caught you.

Even the old leaves of the wintered oak
seem, in this late light, some future hue.
The winds exchange a word in their own tongue.

The leafless trees are black, and yet the horse-dung
heaped up in the fields, a richer black.
Each hour grows younger as it passes through.

The Cry

The call of one lone bird can make us cry –
whatever sounds just once, then dies away.
But listen: beyond the mere sound of their play,
those yelling kids beneath the open sky –

they cry the *chance!* They hammer every scream
like a wedge into the black interstices
of the world – those cracks where only the bird-cries
can pass clean through, the way men do in dreams.

O, where are we now? Freer and freer,
like kites torn from their lines, we loop and race
in the middle air . . . Our tattered hems snicker

like lunatics . . . O lord, make one great choir
of all the criers, so they wake as one voice,
one current, carrying both the head and lyre!

Time

Is there really such thing as time-the-destroyer?
When will it shatter the tower on the rock?
When will that low demiurge overpower
this heart, that runs only to heaven's clock?

Are we really so fragile, so easily broken
as fate wants to prove us, or have us believe?
Is the infinite life that our childhood awakened
torn up by the roots, and then thrown in the grave?

Look how the ghosts of impermanence slide
straight through the mind of the open receiver
again and again, like smoke through a tree.

Among the Eternal – wherein we reside
as that which we truly are, the urgent, the strivers –
we still count; as their means, as their Earth-agency.

Dancer

You were still half a child. You came and went.
But you mapped the dancer in that moment's chance
to the empty constellation of the dance:
that dance in which we fitfully transcend

Nature's dumb order. Only Orpheus
could stir you to the deepest listening:
you were the one still moved from that first song,
and still surprised if a tree took long to choose

whether or not to go along with you.
You knew the old still centre, that clear space
where the lyre was first raised up and rang out true.

For this, you tried to shape the ceremony,
to fit the perfect steps that might one day
turn his own around, might turn his face.

Being

Silent comrade of the distances,
Know that space dilates with your own breath;
ring out, as a bell into the Earth
from the dark rafters of its own high place –

then watch what feeds on you grow strong again.
Learn the transformations through and through:
what in your life has most tormented you?
If the water's sour, turn it into wine.

Our senses cannot fathom this night, so
be the meaning of their strange encounter;
at their crossing, be the radiant centre.

And should the world itself forget your name
say this to the still earth: *I flow.*
Say this to the quick stream: *I am.*

Afterword

The Sonnets to Orpheus were composed in remarkable cir-
cumstances. Rilke had immured himself in the freezing little
Chateau de Muzot, near Sierre in the Rhône valley. He was by
then engaged in his long-anticipated completion of the Duino
Elegies; in the midst of this fever and ferment the Sonnets
arrived as an unasked-for gift. Around the beginning of 1922
the forces that would draw the Sonnets forth had all swung
into alignment: Rilke's lover Merline (the artist Elizabeth Klos-
sowska, who signed herself 'Baladine') had left him a postcard
of a drawing of Orpheus, having earlier given him a transla-
tion of Ovid's *Metamorphoses*; in what seems almost a delib-
erate technical preparation, he had just finished making a
version of Michelangelo's sonnets; and he had taken charge of
the last journals of Vera Ouckama Knoop.

Vera, who had died of leukaemia two years previously, had
been a childhood friend of Rilke's daughter Ruth. She was a
gifted dancer, who earlier had made a powerful impression on
the poet. Vera's mother had sent Rilke the diaries she had kept
towards the end of her illness. The temptation to make the
tragic Vera the Eurydice to his Orpheus was overwhelming.
('His' in both senses: Rilke knew he was singing more clearly
than he ever had, and – feeling himself so strongly in the
god's grip, *one appointed to praise* – at times conflates himself
with the singing god almost unthinkingly. This is self-aston-
ishment as much as it is arrogance, and we forgive this as eas-
ily as we forgive Dante his vanities in the *Commedia*.)
Besides, one can also read the Sonnets as a love poem; the
original dedication, barbarously omitted from this volume,
was *Geschrieben als ein Grab-mal fur Wera Ouckama Knoop*
('written as a grave-monument for Vera Ouckama Knoop').

That such a work should be dedicated to a woman Rilke did not know particularly well indicates a straightforward case of human infatuation.

In this state of high exhilaration, Rilke – barely able to cut the channel fast or deep enough to catch the overflow from this long-anticipated dam-burst – began to write his Sonnets. Fifty-four poems were composed in two short bursts, amounting in total to a period of thirteen days. One poem was added later, possibly for numerological reasons, although I've no proof of this. Fifty-five (like thirteen) is a Fibonacci number, and intimately related to the Golden Ratio, of which the off-centre break in the sonnet form is the most obvious literary manifestation. If one were to reduce the 'essence of the sonnet' to a geometrical description, one might call it a square of text divided horizontally at, roughly, the golden section; though I'm obliged to add that, as self-evident as this seems to me, this is hardly uncontroversial. However, as the Sonnets themselves also constitute a kind of meta-essay on the possibilities of the sonnet form, I'd be surprised if the opportunity to inscribe its signature motif in the broad structure of the work hadn't occurred to Rilke.

Thirteen days is a preposterously brief period of time for the composition of such a substantial and technically demanding sequence, and Rilke's feat has very few if any precedents in Western literature. This it to say such inspirations are *not normal*, and are usually found only in naïfs and doggerelists; but in Rilke's defence, he was not a normal man. His mind, at times, resembles nothing so much as that of a giant articulate insect. He described the experience of writing the Sonnets as 'enigmatic dictation', and indeed working at that speed, it could not have felt otherwise. In an earlier age we would have had no trouble in describing the Sonnets – in the manner of their composition, their lucid vision of the future, their oracular turn of phrase – as a prophetic book. Which would make Rilke a prophet of sorts; perhaps a fair description, if what you mean by prophet is someone so sensitive that they become not only a lightning rod for all the crackling static of the culture, but also a satellite-dish, a 'receiver' (to use a Rilkean favourite) for things a less precisely attuned and calibrated sensibility would never be aware of. These individuals possess no supernatural powers, but do have an abnormally strong sense of what's on the wind for us.

With the Sonnets, though, Rilke was flying his kite in a thunderstorm. Certain kinds of art practice are constitutionally dangerous. We are real objects in the universe, and so just as affected by vibration as anything else; however, we continually act as if we're immune, and tend to dismiss the 'sufferings of the artist' as either mere drama-queenery or, at best, neurotic excess. They can be both those things, certainly; but artists also put themselves in the way of a dangerous kind of sympathetic resonance. (Of which Rilke writes approvingly, and rather unwisely, in 'be the glass that shatters with its own ringing'. '*Zerschlug*' I was tempted to render as 'shiver' or 'tremble', as a shattered glass is no use to anyone.)

So it may have proved with the Sonnets, whose revelation Rilke's mind may not have had time to prepare a home for. Who knows what remote and inhuman harmony Rilke inadvertently conducted in their composition; but my hunch is that, even mediated, tamed and humanised by his great formal mastery, it probably still killed him, even if the effects were delayed: the mind is part of the body, and they share one another's ills. (And before you dismiss this somewhat romantic theory, remember the preposterous sensitivity of the man. He could not bear to be in same room as a dog: not because he hated them, but because he loved them too much. He detested the way we have made them so needful of us, so *patheticated*, and said of them that 'we have raised them up to a soul for which there is no heaven'.)

Either way, Rilke had soon followed his Eurydice – dying, like her, of leukaemia, at the end of the December of 1926, almost five years to the day after that on which he had he received her last diaries. His own gravestone bears the astonishing inscription he had written the year before his death: *Rose, oh reiner Widerspruch, Lust, Niemandes Schlaf zu sein under soviel Lidern* – 'Rose, oh pure contradiction, joy, no one's sleep under so many lids', though untranslatable are the puns on *reiner* (solipsist to the end that he was) and on *Lidern / Liedern*. In his rose-poem in the Sonnets, Rilke speaks of 'impossible richness, silk dress on silk dress / laid upon a body of pure light'. Below the layers of song upon song upon song, there was nothing but the radiant nothingness to which he saw himself returned, and from which the song would emerge again, in the mouth of another Orpheus.

> Raise no stone to his memory. Just let
> the rose put forth each year, for his name's sake:
> Orpheus. Perhaps we'll find him take
> the shape of this, and then of that – and yet
> we need no other name: *Orpheus*, we say
> wherever the true song is manifest.

*

The placing of the work in its biographical context is of course secondary to the discussion of the work itself – tertiary, even, since all the issues of style, aesthetic and interpretation which form the bulk of serious criticism are secondary already. As important as all these things are, they nonetheless do not engage directly with the poem, which is now rarely treated as a direct and trustworthy form of human discourse. This is in part down to our blind subscription to the Modernist dictum which states that a poem has little paraphrasable sense – little sense at all, indeed, beyond that which inheres only in the unique form of words the poem has won for itself. Granted its uniquely expressed sense, the poem must be then *interpreted*, if we are to work out what it means; and by the time we work out what the poem means, no one has any energy left to discuss what that meaning might propose. In its cruder manifestations, this approach does little more than foster a fundamental distrust of the poem as something in which meaning has been deliberately withheld.

The 'necessary oracularity' of the poem – forced into its wildly original speech by its heroic attempts to articulate the inarticulable – is a pernicious half-truth. It leaves us with poetry that can only be talked around and about, but not *with*. The Sonnets, for all their occasional obscurity, also make a great deal of plain sense. This sense has to be placed at the heart of any discussion if the poems are actually to be *useful* to us, and perhaps at the heart of all discussion of poetry if we are to both legitimise and encourage its original thinking as well as its original speech – and attend to some of the very considerable thinking that poetry *has* been doing over the last century.

My main motivation in making this version was selfish. I wanted to make a rhymed English version for my own use, one that would, hopefully, have just a little of the self-sufficiency of the German – meaning one I could memorise, and carry round in my head. Over the last twenty-five years, I've undergone a long and at times painful conversion to scientific materialism. The abolition of God was one matter, but his vast retinue of fairies and pixies (in my own case, this would include everything from ghost, soul and superstition to the seductive appeals of essentialism, humanism and the Anthropic Principle-end of intelligent design) were considerably more difficult to kill off.

[65]

Accomplishing this gave me some satisfaction, but it left the room terribly quiet and empty. I then sought some text I might get in my head as a vade mecum, whereby I could simply remember what I now held to be most true. I'd required this for my beliefs in the past, before my scepticism had managed to chase them all from the house. It was a surprise to find that the best candidate was a poem I already knew pretty well.

However, I was then rather dismayed to discover the Sonnets' recent recruitment to the cause of 'spiritual literature'. These days, this tends to denote a genre with no practical application beyond the invocation of a sort of diffuse and torpid sense of well-being, amounting to – more sinisterly – little more than a sort of generalised call to political inaction (one reason, perhaps, that its self-centred woolliness has received so little discouragement). I suppose one positive outcome has been to leave the likes of the Dao Te Ching and the Dhammapada looking like the plain-speaking manuals of practical instruction they always were; but the Sonnets have a just such a clear pragmatism about them too.

Despite their continual invocation of the Singing God, and the vague pantheism Rilke occasionally conjures as symbolic of the connection we have lost to the Earth, the Sonnets are a strongly non-religious work, and easily capable of an anti-religious interpretation. Though Rilke's myth – all half-light and demiurge – smacks of Gnosticism, he was not religious, and strove to locate all his spiritual wonder in the life we lead now.

The two principal religious errors seem to me beautifully refuted in the Sonnets. The first is to think of truth as being in the possession of an inscrutable third party, whose knowledge and intentions can only be divined. However, we are all the thinking that matter is doing in this part of the universe. If the universe has an eye, it sees only through the eyes on this Earth and elsewhere; if a mind, it thinks only in these minds. Truth, therefore, is not determined (a subtle error, which posits its alternative residence) but sensibly, unilaterally, and provisionally *decided*. Science proceeds not on certainty, but on the basis of best-working and falsifiable hypothesis. Only belief and religion have certainties, or at least insist on maintaining faith in them; and if scepticism is sanity, certainty is its opposite. The Sonnets insist on sheer wondering enquiry as *the* central sane human activity, a way of configuring our most honest prepositional stance towards the universe. Significantly, they contain around sixty different questions: *But is that true? Do we know it or do we not? Do you dare give it a name? Who knows all the losses of the Earth?*

The second error is to think of any afterlife or any reincarnation we are bound for as more extraordinary than finding ourselves here in the first place. This projection of ourselves into a future beyond our deaths warps our actions in, and therefore our sense of responsibility to, the here and now – as well as our negotiations with the real beings with whom we share and to whom we will bequeath a home. ('To whom we will bequeath the Earth' is of course an idiotic way of putting it these days, given it is now radiantly clear that it is not the Earth that needs saving – the Earth will cheerfully flick us off like ash on its sleeve – but ourselves.) This, in a perfectly straightforward sense, is *already* life after death, as remarkably so as any 'you' you might wake as in the future. Factor out the illusion of the unitary self – being a phantom centre created by an evolutionary necessity – and its back-formations of ego and soul, and being here once is the identically equivalent miracle to being here again. Human religion's demotion of this astonishing situation to the status of existential preamble is in some ways its supreme accomplishment. Religion acts as if it holds copyright on the miraculous, and yet is dedicated to eradicating the *real* wonder from the human experience. In the Sonnets, being here '. . . is a source / with a thousand well-heads; a net of pure force / that no one can touch and not kneel down in awe'.

I'd summarise the informing insight of the Sonnets as follows. Man is probably unique amongst the mammals in that he has conscious foreknowledge of his own death. Knowing he will die means he acts, in part, as if he were already dead, already historical – having conducted the imaginative exercise so often it is engraved on his mind by the time he is five or six years old. From a young age, then, this knowledge consciously or unconsciously leads the future-producing mechanism of his mind to construct his life as an authentic and intelligible narrative – i.e. one possessive of meaning, one whose meaning he can overview, and one whose meaning will survive his physical death. He has become so accustomed to living in death's shadow that it is wholly natural for him to do so; he barely notices that, while contingency and fate might shape his life, it is death that drives its plot. Like Orpheus, he too has descended to the land of the shades, and then done what no beast has until now had the *permission* to do: return to the living present. His condition is therefore existentially transgressive (another factor that feeds into his great capacity for self-loathing), but his ghosthood status – his ability to send his mind ahead of him, flying through walls, through skin and fur, over interstellar distances, into alien elements – informs his behaviour in positive ways too: for one thing, he is the only animal capable of imaginative empathy with any other species, and for all his monstrous rapacity, perhaps the first Earth has known that can operate against the Darwinian imperative of blind self-interest. Nonetheless his condition is more riven than dual, and more than one philosopher has described human consciousness as a crime against nature.

[68]

Rilke had a vision of Orpheus as the ideal resolution of this potentially intolerable schism. Orpheus was a man who had found the perfect balance between death and life, eternity and the living present, by singing across the gap and inhabiting both at once. The Sonnets imply that how well a man or woman deals with their twin citizenship determines the degree of their authenticity; and in Orpheus, Rilke sees the ideal possessor of the 'double realm'. He knows that the answer is to live in the heart of the paradox itself, to form a stereoscopic view of the world with one eye in the land of the living and one eye in the land of the dead, in the breathing present and in atemporal eternity. 'But he can raise the dead / and conjured through his half-transparent lids / confuses their dark land in everything.'

Both evidence and celebration of this state of ghosthood is our *singing*. To sing as a human is not to sing as birds sing; as birds sing, humans talk. For a human, to sing is to do something unique and with no analogue in other species. It is to unite the discrete quanta of passing time through music and lyric. These things offer a stay against time's passing. Music weaves a line through the discontinuous present (we now have some proof that our brains appear to measure out time in three-second sections – approximate to the default human line-length of poetry, being the perfect 'mnemonic slot'); lyric unites the time-based events of our words by recalling them back into the presence of one another through the repetition of their sounds. By continually returning us to the previous moment, the lyre cheats that time which carries us to our deaths, and insists that time also has a cyclical aspect. 'Is there really such thing as time-the-destroyer?' The endless river rolls on, but through song we can row against the current and arrest, for a little while, our own progress. Time is a little collapsed into no-time, and we lose some sense of its passing;

through the song, we are reunited with our truest state of being, that of serene ghosthood. This finds its most integrated expression in the yin-yang weave of the song and the dance (identified in the Sonnets with Orpheus and Eurydice, but the germ of the myth is deeper and ungendered), unified idea and rhythmic action, being and passing, endlessly drawing one another forth.

> And should the world itself forget your name
> say this to the still earth: *I flow*.
> Say this to the quick stream: *I am*.

To sing is also to praise. Praise has rightly had a bad press recently, but it can also be an intransitive act, and so Rilke describes it in the Sonnets. Praise need not be rendered to anything but the elements that gave us birth, and the act of praise is simply our closing the loop, making ourselves once again continuous with those elements through the song we share: as Rilke here proposes, if we see ourselves once again as clayborn, we can sing again of what the Earth herself sings. Rilke shows that even just attending mindfully to something as simple as eating an apple can be just such an act of terrestrial continuity: 'This sweet-sharp fire / rising in the taste, to grow / clarified, awake, twin-sensed, / of the sun and earth, the here and the now –'

The singing god Orpheus can also lead us back to that innocent relationship. 'Though at the last, their wrath dismantled you / while your voice was taken up by everything, / the lions, rocks, birds and trees. There it still rings' – wherein we can recognise our own song again. For this, Rilke suggests, we owe the furious jealousy of the Maenads a debt.

The Sonnets also sound a terrible warning. Any animal which develops, as a by-product of its blind evolution, an inwardly-reflected self-image (we need a narrower definition than 'consciousness', which is surely a disease of degree, and which only an outrageous 'species-ism' declares solely a human preserve) might also have reached a fatal evolutionary impasse. It becomes lost in its dream, being essentially the infinite extension of its technological instinct, which we have seen grow from flinthead to cityscape.

That is to say: everywhere we look, we see the world purely in the highly restricted synecdoche of its human *use*. The dream is so powerful, our first instinct is to emphatically deny this is so. (Five minutes' meditation on how strange your shoes look without you in them should do it, though. Now look up: if everything still looks *normal*, you're still sleeping.) Eventually – reinforced by mutual corroboration, and the forceful designations of language – the dream becomes so heavily constructed and all-pervasive that we begin to mistake it for our element. We are then in danger of blithely or accidentally destroying our *real* element and habitat, with which we no longer feel any physical continuity. If our own evolution is in any way typical of the carbon-based life-form, it might explain the terrible silence that presently meets our radio telescopes whichever way we turn them. (We are a fortunate planet, but surely not *that* unique; let's hope that we merely find ourselves in an especially quiet backwater.) Other species are also excluded from our dream; their own elements and dreams are of negligible value to us. 'My dumb friend . . . you are so alone / because of us, each word and sign / we use to make this world our own . . .'

Rilke was also painfully aware of the voracity of the machine, and knew that in erroneously crediting it with its own independent teleology we had created something of a golem – something that, unless we could master it, would doom us by its insatiable appetite, alienating us further from the Earth and from one another.

No one could mistake the timeliness of Rilke's call to confront our own nature, to address our own endangered species – this astonishing double creature of horse and rider, singer and dancer, breath and clay, life and death, noun and verb, being and becoming, *I am* and *I flow*. How in heaven's name are we to live, now the soul we have bred into ourselves no longer has a heaven to ascend to? The word *Earth* is the Sonnets' heartbeat, and is offered as an answer in itself.

[i]

The near-inhuman speed of the Sonnets' composition means that there are occasional imperfections – repetitions, argumentative contortions (a specific hazard of using rhyme while composing so quickly), and obscurities of allusion and sense – that any poet less violently inspired, Rilke included, would probably have ironed out. These are easily forgiven, of course, and merely relics of the poem's conduction, the broken feathers left after a mad and brilliant flight through an extraordinary course. Perhaps the truly great poems *all* contain just such a breathless record of their own composition, and are unthinkable without them.

While these can be translated, they are not, however, something that can be honestly versioned. This is not a translation, but a version. A translation tries to remain true to the original words and their relations, and its primary aim is usually one of stylistic elegance (meaning, essentially, the smooth elimination of syntactic and idiomatic artefacts from the original tongue: a far more subtle project than it sounds) – of which lyric unity is only one of several competing considerations. It glosses the original, but does not try to replace it. Versions, however, are trying to be poems in their own right; while they have the original to serve as detailed ground-plan and elevation, they are trying to build themselves a robust home in a new country, in its vernacular architecture, with local words for its brick and local music for its mortar. This means they must have their own course, their own process, and have to make a virtue of their own human mistakes; they will have, in other words, their *own* pattern of error and lyric felicity. Any attempt to replicate that of the original is perverse in the case of the error, doomed in the case of the felicity, and redundant in terms of the overall project.

Translations can be more-or-less definitive until such point as they fall far enough behind the living speech of the target language to reveal their own archaism or modishness, fashionable style being something our contemporary myopia almost always conceals. In other words, translations date. Free versions, on the other hand, can never be definitive; but nor do they date in quite the same way. While we might find J. B. Leishman's rhymed version of the Sonnets uncomfortably aureate, we can hardly say that Wyatt's interpretations of Petrarch have dated; we recognise that the master he was serving was English lyric, not Petrarch. Petrarch was merely being *used*. (This is no disrespect. While it's an important human courtesy elsewhere, Honouring the Great Poet is a quixotic sentimentality here, and will get us nowhere. On these occasions we should rigorously use their names as metonyms for their texts.) Leishman, on the other hand, was clearly trying to serve two masters, and this always ends in disappointing both.

Both translation and version are also at a rather curious and potentially marvellous advantage: unlike the poem in the source language, fixed for ever in the time and the diction in which it was written, the translated poem can be translated not just into the language but the *culture* of the age, whenever that culture deems it necessary. This strange anomaly – the fact that the translated poem can undergo continuous cultural rebirth, in a way denied to the original – raises the possibility that some poems in translation could, theoretically, end up being *more* central to a culture than that of the language in which they were first conceived. Either way, they demonstrate that the life of the text is not circumscribed by its original incarnation and the influence it may exert on other poems. Even if we believe all poetic translation a fool's errand, the original nonetheless offers a blueprint for a wholly new poem the target language would never have otherwise produced.

[iv]

Charles Simic once memorably remarked that poems are translations from the silence. For a version to be any kind of real poem, it must first reinhabit that extralinguistic silence the original poem once itself enjoyed – which is to say the poem must make a symbolic exit from language altogether. In this meditative space, its pattern of idea and image is reconsumed by its own strangeness, and when it re-emerges into language rediscovers itself in original speech. This is the inevitable answer to the request that *everything* be subservient to a lyric rule. By definition, that subservience insists that you are engaged in an act of versioning, not translation; because you know the original surface-sense will suffer as a consequence of the local exigencies of consonance, rhyme and metre, your allegiance must then switch from the original words to your subjective interpretation of them – to that wholly personal mandala of idea and image and spirit that floats free of the poem, and resides, for a while, only in that symbolic mentalese that functions in an intercessory role in the line's reincarnation. This, I think, corresponds to Roman Jakobson's idea of 'intersemiotic translation' or transmutation, and is perhaps the only occasion we come across this in the verbal medium.

As 'lyric' is a principal theme of the Sonnets, it perhaps merits some brief discussion. Lyric unites words primarily (though not wholly) through the repetition of their sounds; if you believe words to be *indivisibly* part-sound and part-sense, then lyric must also unite sense. Reciprocally, the words we choose to convey the most urgent sense automatically tend to exhibit a higher level of musical organisation. Lyric presents an additional strategy besides syntax to bind our words together. This, incidentally, has severe consequences for the Saussurian dogma of the arbitrariness of the sign, which most poets know to be sheer madness. (As did Saussure, deep down, who ended his days tormented by the demon of anagrams.) This arbitrariness would be fine, if words merely *denoted* – and since science uses language in a purely denotative way, linguisticians understandably tend to throw their weight behind that theory. Poetry is just as interested in what words connote, however, and the overlap between their connotative haloes, their common *feel*, is often strongly manifest in shared features of their sounds.

In one aspect this is simply the magnetism of sounds, through familiar association, to part-arbitrary tongue-specific conventions of usage; but another aspect reveals a broad principle of iconicity, i.e. the shapes of sounds in the mouth naturally formed as physical analogues to the shapes of real things and processes. (The definition of 'iconicity' has been traditionally limited to onomatopoeia alone, but this is slowly changing.) These two aspects are difficult to separate. It's hard, in other words, to establish whether most English words that contain the sound 'unk' carry the connotations 'low' and 'concavity' because they have helplessly converged on an arbitrary English convention – or because, irrelevant of language, there is something in this human sound that mimics a reality. That such features of language resist conventional systematic study certainly does not mean they always will; yet many are still quick to dismiss the poets' very defining strategy as a minor curiosity, as mere 'sound-symbolism'.

Suffice to say that in the lyric manifesto of the Sonnets, an astonishingly coherent German music is offered as best proof of their own argument. Lyric unifies meaning as powerfully as does syntax. Indeed, since lyric is part-music, and music can draw sense from thin air, its use supplies the speech-meaning with precisely that additional music-sense. That sense, how-ever, is of a different nature. Though we experience music as sense-making structure, its sense appears to be intransitive: less that it means nothing, than that its meaning is *so* utterly resistant to paraphrase, we can barely agree on a single w rd to gloss its beautifully articulate statements. But   clearly agree on that meaning so strongly, we feel   elaboration to be superfluous anyway. (Schumann   is response to a query about a piece's *meaning* wa   it again. Works on the aesthetics of music ar   n-spicuous by their absence. Even the subje   ost tautological.) Lyric unites the intransit   and emotional sense of music with the transitive and para-phrasable senses of speech.

Consequently, in a qualified but real sense, one can no more translate a poem than one can a piece of music.

[vi]

However the *operation* of lyric is wholly dependent on hope-lessly, irredeemably tongue-specific phonosemantic coinci-dence. And as a result, the more we work to unify the music in the target language, the more the surface-sense of the lyric-bound original must shift, and the greater the danger we'll end up saying something very different, and possibly even contradictory. The book in your hands is not a 'reliable' version, but no version can be. All we can do is try to make a virtue of the problem, and as far as possible legislate against travesty.

Travesty, alas, is in the eye of the beholder, and the more familiar readers are with original, the greater the likelihood that travesty will be their diagnosis. For that reason I've done as much as I dared in the presentation of this version to distance it from the original. There is no parallel text, and I've given each poem a neutral title, as a small mnemonic handle. Such gestures shouldn't be misinterpreted as claims to definitiveness, or anything else; indeed I can make no especial claims for this version, as versions genuinely *are* abandoned – being ess███████ly exegeses, and so really open-ended enquiries. While for███████ader the act of interpretation should be coterminous wit████████r direct engagement with the poem, interpretation mu█████████de the acts of both versioning and translation; this is d████████████the case of the former.

[vii]

An attempt to be faithful to the *words* of oracular lines – and there are many in the Sonnets - will almost invariably result in something even less comprehensible in the new tongue, and such a faith should therefore be thoroughly interrogated. The act of translating something you don't really understand in German into something you understand even less in English is, at the end of the day, a pretty strange way of passing the time. If a poem has *no* plain sense, however - i.e. no paraphrasable content – and its merits exist purely in its music, its 'vibe' and its pattern of tongue-specific connotation – it cannot be translated other than through an act of faith. No one has agreed an exchange rate. The results might be terrific, but their 'fidelity' is totally unverifiable. (Here one might think of a poet like Paul Celan. A great translator like Richard Howard does not translate 'words', but – as Howard once snapped back at a student – systems of relations between them. Perversely, however, when it comes to those very poets hailed as working at the sophisticated limits of the language, translators are often forced back to the piecemeal business of ticking off the words again.)

[viii]

There are no ghosts, no gods, nothing secretly lurking in the temple of the poem whose vengeful wrath we will incur through our failure to honour it. The author and the critic might reasonably scream *travesty*, but they aren't in the poem either. Any faith in *anything* is misplaced, and masks an essentialist creed. A 'faithful' translation requires an original, a translation and an essence. A poem has no essence. (It has a spirit, but this is utterly subjective and unfixable.) Trust, on the other hand, requires only two terms. So while *faithful* is an impossible judgement, our versions might nonetheless be subjectively reckoned to be trustworthy. The original poem has a consensually agreed paraphrasable sense, and a consensually agreed unparaphrasable sense. We translate the former and imitate the latter.

[ix]

A rhymed version is by definition a forcefully interpretive project. This is a matter of pure statistics. In the composition of an original poem, there is no real difference between form and content, since both are part of the same dynamic process. The fact that they can be later distinguished lies about the manner of the poem's composition. Inscribed in the initial germ of content – those few 'inspired' words we get for free – is the form that will realise its most effective expression; that form then becomes the engine which then draws content from the mind; thereafter – or at least when the poet is working at full tilt – they alternate as rapidly and indivisibly as an electromagnetic wave, changing and modifying one another as they go. In a version, however, the content has already been supplied. There can be – within the brutal constraints of predetermined content, predetermined form and predetermined conventions of natural syntax – nothing like the fluidity needed to create *anything* resembling a real poem.

If the content tries to stay fixed, the rhymes will merely be *inflicted*, and will be a disaster. Rhyme is the insertion of a heavily foregrounded word at the end of the line which must usually be naturalised by everything that precedes it. In an original poem the rhyme often not only dictates the syntax, but a large part of the content. Rhyme implies a compositional fluidity of sense; in a real poem, that sense is infinitely fluid, as there is no original to betray – and so it can be cheerfully *determined*, in part, by the hunt for the rhymes themselves. In a version, that fluidity has to be carefully negotiated. If rhymes are to be used – especially in a rhyme-poor target language – *then some aspect of the content must change.* The attempt in the act of translation to honour *both* the form and content of the original is a precise recipe for translationese, where the final 'given', the natural syntax of the target language, is forced to bear the brunt of the entire problem and buckles under the pressure. (This is a more depressing diagnosis than attributing these manglings to calques from the original syntax – through which we can at least sometimes project into the poem an attractive whiff of the foreign and exotic.)

Content-translation can of course take the strategic form of one-to-one synonymy if we were dealing with individual words; but if we take Richard Howard's advice, it's the unity of the individual phrase we should be trying to render, and here we are forced into a complex disease-of-degree game: the metonymic substitution of the original sense with its interpretation. The felicity or veracity of these substitutions is inevitably and definitively *subjective*, for both writer and reader.

[x]

Most of the trouble in this business stems from a failure to articulate the project and communicate that explicitly to the reader – or the reader's wilful or inept misinterpretation of that project. If a translation is read as a version, or a version as a translation, the result is disappointment and confusion. Translations fail when they misrepresent the language of the original, or fail to honour the rules of natural syntax. Versions fail when they misrepresent the *spirit* of the original, or fail in any one of the thousand other ways bad poems fail. If, through naïvety or over-ambition, both translation and version are attempted simultaneously, the result is foredoomed. Essentially, if we are not prepared to make a choice between honouring the word or the spirit, we are likely to come away with nothing. Or, perhaps, between method and goal: in translation, the integrity of the means justifies the end; in the version, the integrity of the end justifies the means.

[xi]

Until now I've resisted the following admission on the grounds of self-incrimination – but while I can read a very little of a few languages, I am simply no linguist of any kind. While this would naturally make 'translation' an impossible project, it does not, I believe, rule out the version. If I waver (as I constantly do) in this belief, I can always supply myself with a couple of stones' worth of evidence from my shelves that, in the translation of poetry, even a very *good* acquaintance with the source language is no guarantee of anything at all. At least the ignorant monoglots tend to triangulate their version from multiple cribs for fear of missing anything, for fear of missing *everything*; whereas the fluent tend to work from one, their own – which might be no better (and is often worse) than those available from other sources. Paradoxically, the best-qualified – the bilingual – have no need nor selfish urge to translate at all. If they do, they do so for money, or as a service to the rest of us.

[xii]

So mere fluency in the source language is not enough. Poetic nuance is what makes a good line; poetic nuance – which no single literal crib can ever capture, but several might converge upon – lies in the last percentile of idiomatic speech, that is to say the part that lies between mere fluency and absolute command. Besides, even in the matter of conducting the plain sense, it's easy to give examples from translators whose less-than-perfect qualifications were, in the end, only the source of the overconfidence which amplified their error. When reading J. B. Leishman's version, for example, I came across the following (from the poem presented here as 'The Sarcophagi in Rome'): 'Sarcophagi (How my thoughts of you throng / to the heart of all my greeting and praise!), / whom the joyful water of Roman days / transforms in transfluent song. / Or those others, candid and open as eyes / of shepherd happily stirring, /

within full of stillness and honeyed thighs, / whence came ravished butterflies whirring.'

All this talk of honeyed thighs and ravished butterflies intrigued me, but not in a good way. Looking at the original, even *my* German made it clear that that Leishman, in his tearing hurry, had misread *bienensaug* ('bee-suck', a plant-name I'd seen translated elsewhere as 'honeysuckle') as *beinensaug* ('leg-suck'); and then compounded this error tenfold by making it his rhyme word, 'honeyed thighs', the 'honeyed' possibly influenced by 'honeysuckle', though heaven knows why. (The word turned out to be one of several common names for *Lamium album*, the white dead-nettle.) Leishman's version is in better English than many rhymed versions, but this was achieved by negotiating away almost every other consideration, including the original's plain sense, for the sake of achieving a natural rhyme.

[xiii]

At the end of the day, everyone is bound to valorise their own expertise (hence, I suppose, my flailing attempts to present my ignorance as some kind of state of grace), and absolutely none of this will convince those who have studied hard to achieve a fluency that their hard-won skill might count for relatively little in the *literary* (as opposed to . . . fideistic) merit of their version. But the translation and the version can be thought of as separate parts of a linear sequence, the first expert operation, the second intuitive process – and they need not be carried out by the same organism. Little is lost by them being the work of two individuals, when a great deal of perspective and humility may be lost by them being carried out by one. The only incontrovertibly superior qualification is held by those who are both *genuinely* bilingual *and* gifted poets; but this skill-set is mere freakish coincidence, and the likes of the Anglo-German Michael Hofmann or the Anglo-Hungarian George Szirtes are few and far between. However, in the work of those writers we are entitled to trust a little more that our untranslatable nuance has found a more fit analogue in the target language than usual, since the two languages *and* the poetic machinery occupy the same head – and are therefore, one presumes, all in closer dialogue.

[xiv]

Versioning allows a poet to disown their own voice and try on another. This voice might fit well, or might fit badly. When the poet returns to reclaim their old voice, it either no longer quite fits, or has altered, having apparently kept some strange company of its own in the meantime. Sometimes it has just disappeared. None of this is ever regretted. The voice isn't you, and never was – or if it *was* you, it was all there was of you. Now where does that leave you? Who was that masked man?

Acknowledgements

Thanks are due to the editors of the following publications, where many of these poems first appeared: *London Review of Books*; *Poetry*; *Poetry Review*; *Oxford Poetry*; *The Yellow Nib*; *Magma*.

I can't work without music, and have always found that music can help unlock a particular lyric or argumentative problem. I'll resist giving you the playlist for this book, but am compelled to mention Herbert Henck's astonishing recording of Federico Mompou's *Musica Callada* (the phrase derives from Juan de la Cruz), for which discovery I am grateful to John Gray. Henck's reading makes explicit the great subtlety of Mompou's musical argument; it seemed to me to represent a perfect analogue to the Sonnets, its language at once lyric and algebraic, direct and mystical, expressive and impersonal.

I am indebted to the many other translators of the Sonnets from whom I have freely and shamelessly adapted lines when theirs presented the better solution, but in particular to Edward Snow, whose miraculously clear translation I would heartily recommend to anyone interested in the actual *language* Rilke used. Stephen Cohn's wonderfully detailed notes to his own version were invaluable, even if I often ended up ignoring their sound direction. Thanks are also due to Paul Keegan and Matthew Hollis for their meticulous reading; to the friends who read these versions in earlier drafts, in particular Jo Shapcott, David Harsent, Andrew Greig and John Glenday; and especially to Hannah Griffiths and Kathleen Jamie for their encouragement and wise advice. Lastly, I suppose I should thank Michael Donaghy for finally letting us all get a word in edgeways (but such *lengths*, Spike).

Kirriemuir, April 2006